NLP EXPERT

Explosive Techniques Of Real Neuro Linguistic Programming. How To Drastically Influence Others And How To Transform Our State Instantly, ¡In Less Than 5 Minutes!

D1520185

ALLAN TREVOR

As a token of appreciation for the trust you have placed in this reading, I would like to offer you a powerful resource completely FREE:

<< Click here to download the book "Dark Psychology And Hypnosis " for FREE >>

This book is specifically designed to unlock all the secrets of persuasive communication. You can become a speaker with great hypnotic influence. In fact, you will be surprised to find that the more you read the secret patterns in this book, the greater your ability to inadvertently persuade others.

<< Click here to download the book "Dark Psychology And Hypnosis " for FREE >>

Or you can also download it from the following QR code:

Content

BRUTAL NLP

Chapter *1*

Elementary concepts of NLP

What is NLP?

Neurolinguistic Programming (NLP) is a communication model that shows us human behavior in detail. It teaches how we do what we do, as well as the strategies that we follow within us to have a particular emotion, be it joy, sadness, euphoria or anger, that prompts us to act and finally to achieve a certain result, and not another.

It is a model, not a theory, and therefore its task is to model what works, not to make theories or connect with psychological or philosophical systems or approaches.

Part of this is that if we know what successful people use unconsciously, we can learn to apply those strategies consciously to achieve success in our work or emotional states.

NLP has tools and skills to develop states of excellence for communication and thus produce changes. Throughout the following pages we will see how it influences us and how it applies to others.

Important principles of NLP in human nature

At first NLP researchers studied therapists who were good at their job. One of the first therapists to be studied was Fritz Perls, who developed the Gestalt therapy of "being here and now." He had a natural gift for reading body language and getting information from the other person immediately.

He focused on the direct opposite of psychoanalysis, which required years of work and self-study to fully understand how someone becomes who they are.

Virginia Satir was the second therapist studied, who developed family therapy in her area. She was not dedicated to working with the problematic person in the family, but rather working with the entire family nucleus.

He said that each behavior and action were part of the family dynamic. He discovered that if he addressed only one person, the family structure would return him to the same situation over and over again, which is why working with the whole family was so important.

The third person the NLP pioneers studied was Milton Erickson, a physician who developed clinical hypnotherapy, with a totally different approach than Perls and Satir, a true genius, who produced results that seemed like magic.

The other was a man named Moshe Feldenkrais, who was in charge of healing the body with an incredible healing that he achieved with his hands.

The underlying operating principles of NLP, called "presuppositions", show the underlying unifying beliefs of these 4 key individuals who were studied to discover the most effective and this ended up becoming the foundations of NLP.

All of these experts agreed on most essential beliefs about human nature. We will mention two of the most important beliefs. The first one is:

1. THERE IS NO INTERNAL ENEMY

There is no monster inside you that is against you. Those beliefs where you feel that you are broken or with an internal enemy, you can take them out of yourself. When people act by hurting themselves in some way, such as drinking too much alcohol or committing a violent crime, they do so because they believe it is necessary for them.

Some of these behaviors may not be sane for most of us, but you have to understand that person's worldview, what goes through their mind, because it will be what prompts them to do what they do.

The second belief is:

2. BEHIND EVERY BEHAVIOR THERE IS A POSITIVE INTENTION

Let's take an example in your own flesh: you see a person, and when you do it your legs shake and the voice breaks, why does it happen? It is not that there is something wrong with you, it is your mind that says that if you face that person something bad could happen, and it protects you so that you survive with these warning signs, so that you avoid confrontation.

With NLP it is possible to observe through the mind to identify what pattern is operating to produce a certain response and then work it to change.

Keep in mind that there is no enemy within you that works against you and that behind each behavior there is always a positive intention. Your mind operates in the best way it knows right now, but it may need adjustments since most brains are programmed between 2 and 5 years of age, and unless we change the software we installed at that time, we will continue to reproduce the same behavior patterns on autopilot, almost without realizing it.

What is the power of use of NLP?

There are many reasons to study NLP, mainly to know how human nature works or to know how you think of yourself. The goal is for us to apply it in the real world where these skill sets make a significant difference.

NLP is extremely necessary today. We are in a world in constant technological evolution, we connect all the time with people we work with, love, important people. We live busy giving answers that we hardly even think about.

In the following pages, you will discover patterns of thought and learn to manage them both for yourself and to manage others.

You will learn a new way of dealing with people and understanding what they think and feel.

Understanding how our mind works

We all have the same wiring in the central nervous system, we learn many of the same things and in the same way, maybe we worry about similar topics, however we do not all think the same. Everyone thinks differently, we are all unique just like our fingerprint.

Without realizing it, we spend our lives getting used to little annoyances and emotional and mental limits. Each of us must establish and protect limits, this is how we create personal feelings of security and we get other people to respect our choices.

Actions such as being able to speak in public, change bad habits for better ones, be more responsible in some matters, we can all be more than we are now, but many give up shortly after trying, saying that "old parrot does not learn to speak ", But that's not true.

It just takes the right tools to do it. By discovering the thought patterns, you can go in and make the appropriate changes. The best way to achieve change is by understanding how feelings were created and working to change them.

How do we create our feelings?

They are born with a stimulus, for example when you wake up, you feel the coffee maker working and the aroma of coffee, a crying child, a dog that barks and you have to take it for a walk, the recent news on the favorite site, or the television on. All these events are stimulations that happen in your brain.

As soon as this information arrives, it is interpreted, you give it a meaning that has an emotion. You gave this feeling. You can see it as a good thing, the dog happy to see you, the coffee maker whistling, the child who cries but who with love will shut up in a moment, a great day awaits you, or you feel anger because the noisy dog does not shut up, the child does not stop. crying and the coffee maker has no coffee.

Either of the two scenarios are stimuli, they have meaning and emotion and this generates a certain reaction. By understanding emotions and the meaning you give to thoughts, you can go back to that thought and work to change it. You can, for example, write down the thoughts and then choose better answers.

The issue here is that many times we are only aware of the first stimulus, then the meaning of the emotion that we associate with said stimulus is outside our consciousness. Try saying things like:

"I feel good when I'm around you."

"You made me angry".

"That client ruined my day."

Despite how these phrases are formulated, the real cause of my emotions is NOT the other person. We are always the ones who give meaning to any situation we live in. Other people or the environment itself do not cause a certain emotional state in us, there is no cause-effect relationship. The proof of this is that the same situation produces different emotional states in different people.
In this sense, no one can cause a certain emotion in us. What happens is that someone exercises an action, and through my internal dialogue I decide to associate an emotion with that action. Ultimately, we are responsible for our emotional state at all times, not the circumstances.

The worlds within our mind

Maybe you know what is real and what is not. Let's see this, you have a twin brother, you both live in the same room, maybe you suppose that the world you live in is the same one that your brother lives in, but no, it is not like that.

Since we are born we notice things, at the beginning there is only chaos, all that information that is not understood flooding the mind, so many images, sounds, smells, tastes, bodily sensations. The mind begins to order everything, to give it languages, the only way it can think is with images, sounds, tastes, feelings and smells. They are cornerstones in the mind.

The world you see and live is really in your head, in no one else's. Your mind creates the world you live in, the relationships you have, the way you act with others, how you feel about yourself, and the filters you create.

Your brain has sight, hearing, sensations, taste and smell, but it does not use them with the same intensity. Later you will understand better what I am talking about.

Discovery activity what is your inner world like?

Look at those clothes you wear, the way you put them on, how you got them out of the closet. In short, the whole process to finally have it on. Now think about the clothes you put on yesterday, with this you recover that data and feel what you experienced while you were wearing them. The mind built that image for you.

Remembering that image is not necessarily the same as yesterday, because it is marked by everything you felt in each situation. You must have a door at the entrance of the house, now that you read this, you thought of your door. You know that, because you live there, imagine that door thoroughly. Now that you have it in mind, open it, the characteristic sound that it makes when you open it arrives. Feel the force you exert when you open it, whether it is soft as a feather in the wind or heavy because it drags on the ground.

Think slowly about all this, each sensation, the information that you have stored and automatically. You will see that you have a lot of information stored.

Now think of the mountains, you are in a field, there is grass, you are lying on your back, your elbow is touching the damp earth. If you are right-handed, imagine that it is the left elbow and vice versa, now try to scratch something with that elbow that is not the one with the most ability. Try to make the initial of your name, to be able to do it you have to imagine that initial letter of your name. While you read this you saw the letter marking the ground, surely you saw the grass damaged by your action. But before all this, you first saw the lyrics in your mind.

How do you see that letter? Some may see it in print, others as a neon sign, a billboard, or a gothic letter. Your mind saw all of this, down to how to write with your nondominant elbow.

Think of other doors, think of the beach, of common places in your day to day, smells associated with doors that you open, sounds that you hear as soon as you enter home or work. When you think about each of these, you feel different emotions, such as the smell of the door behind the dentist's office that scares you, or the smell of freshly applied perfume, when you walk through the door that leads to the bed where that loved one is waiting. , for which you feel pleasure and happiness. Each site has different emotions, pleasant, unpleasant and in many cases neutral. They are a whole world of sensations that enter your brain with a lot of information.

The brain has the ability to classify and archive all this information. It stores everything you have thought, seen, felt, heard or imagined.

The power of anchors

Anchors bring us memories of events and can be changed for better or for worse. They have great power, because they give us access to that strength or weakness. This is where all the senses dealt with in the previous section enter.

We all use anchors on a daily basis. It is an association that is created in certain thoughts, sensations, states and stimuli. Creating anchors in ourselves or in others consists of two phases. First, the person is put in the state where they want to anchor and that exclusive stimulus is given. Another way is to ask him to remember a moment where he felt a state that you would like to arouse at will, there the person reacts in all his senses and that is when the specific stimulus is given several times, for example a pressure on an arm.

Think of that moment in your life where you felt determined and secure, step into the situation and fully associate with it. Relive that experience and when you relive this totally press some part of your body and say "I can". Now think of another similar situation and when you are at the top, do the same. Repeat about seven times so that you have a lot of powerful anchors in you. Now think about that key decision you want to make and launch the anchor signal. That's how easy it is with you.

An easy way for another to have an anchor, it can be by auditory, for example, you are a trainer, in a part of your sports routine, you put a tabata with certain music, all the people who train already have the anchor that now comes that particular set of exercises with so many seconds of action and so many seconds of rest. That is a simple anchor.

What are metaprograms?

The metaprograms are like filters through which we process reality and we create our mental maps. Our brain processes a lot of information with metaprograms that we organize with structures and helps us prioritize. So we can build rapport and generate better communications.

Let's take a brief look at each filter of the metaprograms so that you have a clearer idea of what they are about:

Moving away / Approaching

Moving away: This class of people tend to avoid and recognize problems, they tend to focus on the negative. For them you have to use phrases that have a negative:

"If you don't do your homework, you will get a bad grade"

Approaching: they are people who speak in achievement, in issues, in scope. They generally focus on the positive, with them you talk positive:

"We want to earn more this quarter ...".

Global / Details

Global: They have a more panoramic view of things, for them it is spoken more or less like this:

"In general, this looks like ...".

Details: As the name says, they look at the small details, they should be spoken like this:

"For the month of May, the focus is to achieve 23.5% of ..."

Internal / external

Internal: With them you have to focus on the inside, using your feelings and self-control. They like to make decisions, with them you talk:

"It all depends on you, decide."

External: They are people dependent on others, feel that others control and need feedback. You should talk to them more or less like this:

"Things like this, it has worked for others ...".

Past-oriented / Future-oriented

Oriented to the past: they tend to focus on the past, for with them words about the past should be used:

"Last year when I spoke to ...".

Facing the future: they tend to focus on the future, with them words about the future should be used:

"For next week we will have a new project"

Options / Procedures

Choices: They are people who tend to try new things and focus on choosing. They appreciate variety, they start a lot of things, but they don't always finish them. Words about options should be used with them:

"You can decide what you want ...".

Procedures: they are people with rules, with clear instructions, they respect the rules, for them it is necessary to use phrases about clear procedures:

"You must start from step 1 to 9 to ...".

Proactive / Reactive

Proactive: They are people who enjoy doing things, controlling and undertaking. They love being in charge. For them it is necessary to use phrases related to the action:

"You have to act now ...".

Reactive: they wait for others to lead, analyze objectives and possibilities. To talk to them, use phrases related to waiting:

"Wait for the boss to respond to ...".

Rapport

Rapport or tuning are essential to achieve effective communications. Many times it is achieved intuitively, you have to see how the other person reacts to what you say and gradually discover keywords that cause a reaction. Although it is not only with what is said, body language also plays a big role.

To rapport you have to be aware of how others communicate and how they make gestures, what is their tone of voice, body positions, etc. It is about making coincidence and reflection, imitating without disrespecting the position of the other, to mirror oneself.

If you see a recent dating couple, you will see that they unconsciously copy body positions. You can do the experiment, while you are talking with another person, when she talks about something pleasant for her, imitates her body gestures and position, then, modify the behavior and do the opposite, wait a little and then repeat imitating her gestures. There you are doing rapport.

Beliefs and how to weaken them

Beliefs are judgments and evaluations about ourselves and others. In NLP, generalizations firmly rooted in causality are considered.

Most of the memories were manufactured by your mind to adjust to the thoughts. You remember what you want to remember in each situation.

When you want to persuade others, you may come across memories made by their mind, beliefs that get in the way of your message. You have to weaken those beliefs.

Speaking of beliefs, meet Roger Bannister, who set a record for running a mile in less than 4 minutes. Before such a feat was believed impossible, he took nine years to prepare and err until he succeeded. After he did, they broke that barrier six weeks later, and over the next nine years more than 200 people broke the record. That belief was shattered.

One way to change belief is to associate strong pain with the old belief and immense pleasure with the new one. You may wonder how ridiculous or absurd the belief is, or from whom you learned that, the cost of not removing it from your life. Give that pain a name and change the belief for another.

For example "I don't know how to dance, I have two left feet", those who think like this will never be the life of the party and will warm the seat while others enjoy. Breaking the belief is looking for someone to teach you to dance, enter school and eliminate everything that scares you of ridicule.

Another way to break beliefs is to come up with examples. That is an experience or piece of information that does not fit a generalization of the world. They are a way of questioning beliefs, you are questioning universality and you have a better picture. You give with universal terms, like "everyone, never, always, nobody" just as nobody had been able to run as much as Bannister did.

BRUTAL NLP

_Chapter_2

Mind management Who guides you?

Imagin that you get into a taxi and tell the driver not to take you to a certain place. It sounds strange but many times this is our life.

This is precisely what will be discussed in this chapter, to better understand the consistency of our actions and know where we want to go.

In the processes of NLP is the results framework, where elements that make up valuable goals and that help to maximize the possibility of achieving what we want are addressed.

Let's learn to have a better control of the mind and to know who really guides us.

Define your goal Where do you want to go?

In NLP there is the assumption that everyone can do something, and they only have to find the how. If you can find the way, you will have results and you will know that you are on the right track.

This is very useful when you apply it to what you want, when you want to make big changes and you have stuck or when you just want to make adjustments to some goals that you have or are pursuing.

To achieve this you have to ask yourself key questions:

- What do you want to achieve specifically?
- Where, when, with whom and under what circumstances do you want to achieve the result?
- What prevents you from having that result already?
- What resources do you need to help you create what you want?
- How are you going to get there and what is the first step to achieve this result?

What do you want to achieve specifically?

It is to know the problem, desire or objective. It is formulated in positive, controlled by you, and it has to be clear.

"I don't want to feel upset."

This is not an objective, it is a statement. Likewise, speaking negatively is not processed correctly by the brain. The way to change this is to think of something else, then think:

"Although there may be factors such as a partner, boss, etc., that affect me emotionally, I can feel more persuasive if I am in control."

Know when you will achieve it

You have the most refined goal, now you must have proper evidence. It is seeking a more realistic approach and taking the necessary steps to achieve it.
Is that you put a date:

"I would like to speak more fluent English at the end of the semester."

Where and with whom?
All people are pursuing goals, they spend a large part of their lives in it, when they find it then, they do not feel satisfaction and they go for something else, because that was not what they wanted.

I give you an example, imagine that since you were a child you want to be a doctor, you see on television, in the media, doctors dressed in their gowns, so professional, and it is your dream. To prove yourself you could enter and try, one way is in the Red Cross as a volunteer, seeing what the profession really is like and confirming if you are willing by your passion to give yourself for years to a university career that you will surely exercise for the rest of your life.

What is stopping you from achieving the result already?

There is a double question here, one is the list of action items and the other is what you think and feel.

When you wonder what prevents you from feeling persuasive, you could feel frustration, limited thoughts that stop and need to be worked with focus. Analyze what is real and what does not make it possible to create viable strategies to achieve goals.

The resources you need to help you create it

This is divided into two parts: first the resources you already have and the ones you need. In NLP, resources are knowledge, time, money, experiences, support, contact, etc.

Now you must see what resources you have to feel more persuasive.

You may feel more persuasive telling a success story before you start speaking.

You have to analyze the need, what you need, what you have and how to work with it all.

How are you going to get to the end result?

If you do not take action, the goal is just an idea, you have to have the who, what, how, when and where in spaces you manage.

In NLP, you operate on the premise that having more options is better. The plan where success depends on only one way of doing something is a recipe for failure. A plan is just one route, you have to have more alternate routes.

Mental Duality: Congruence / Incongruity

Surely it has happened to you that you wanted to go somewhere, but also to stay where you were. A part of us that wants to do something and another that does not.

This is incongruity, moments where there is a sense of conflict to reach a goal. It happens in settings like when you want to go to the mountains or to the beach.

When you are in the right moment, with everything going as planned, this is called being in the zone, or being flowing. In NLP it is called congruent. The more aware you are of personal signs of inconsistency, the faster you can identify conflict.

Incongruity is fiction, it takes personal energy to overcome a part of you that opposes a course of action. Much of the emotional and body stress is when the mind tries hard to override the body's desire to prevent it from doing something that violates integrity.

The best thing is that you learn to move in harmony with values. This is how one works to achieve congruence about something that was wanted. Think back to when you were a kid and you wanted that nice toy as a gift and you wanted it with all your heart. Throughout your life you have had many congruent experiences about something desired, things from a book, watching a movie or meeting someone.

Do you live in or out? Associated or dissociated

Associating and disassociating is a useful technique. When you associate yourself with images or experiences, whether they are real or not, the feeling is more intense. When there is dissociation from an experience, we see ourselves in it and we capture much of the information from that image.

When remembering an experience where feelings arise, you are associated with it, while when you imagine and see the feelings from outside, you are dissociated from the experience.

If you feel an unpleasant memory, it would be good if you access the memory in dissociated mode. There is no reason to feel that past experience that hurt you again. However, if you want to do it, you can do it as if it were a movie that you see from the outside, so that the feelings are removed from you and you are only an external spectator of your life. There are people who see everything bad, be it something real or simply imagined, always in associated mode. They literally go to great lengths to feel bad all the time. In addition, they tend to see the pleasant as dissociated. They have changed the way of interpreting things and thus they only ensure depression, bad mood, worry and hopelessness. If you are one of those who interpret reality in this way, I must tell you that you can reverse these habits and do just the opposite. For it,

Maybe you choose to see unpleasant memories, worries, and even visions of the future. It may have already been bad to live them the first time, you don't have to go back to it, to scald yourself. You have no reason to. If that was what they always taught you, you have to unlearn to see everything in a different way, because you know what you like and what you don't like, you know what makes you feel good and what doesn't feel good. You don't have to benefit from constant punishments.

How do we capture reality? Submodalities

Association and dissociation are just part of the subtle distinctions that sensory systems make. In NLP, senses are thought of as modalities and the unique qualities and subtleties within each modality are called submodalities. This reflects how we feel, seeing these as molecules of meaning.

Learning to view memories dissociated can change the experience, figuring out how to play with the other submodalities can greatly change how you feel about something and how you integrate it into thinking about the future.

Now, having the opportunity to find the submodalities of sight, can serve to explore the submodalities of the other senses.

So for the visual case, it refers to brightness, lighting, distance; in the auditory it refers to timbre, tone, volume; if it is about smell it refers to smells and aromas, for taste it refers to bitter, acid, bittersweet and for the kinesthetic modality, weight, texture, etc.

How do you want your day to be? emotional states

Since submodalities influence the past, present, and future, imagine how much more enjoyable and compelling your life could be if you start consciously shaping your day tomorrow. You would make your life easier.

These are valuable questions you could ask yourself each morning:

- What do I expect from this day?
- In the long term, what do I expect? This gives you a sense of direction and purpose.
- Do I do what leads directly to my goals? If not, then you have to explore, to see where productivity is lacking with clearer objectives.
- Am I my best friend and follower right now?
- Am I present in my body, here and now, feeling what I feel, seeing what I see now, listening to what I hear and enjoying the gift of life?

Maybe you often think about the uncertain future, but what you should do is go back to the now, think about the present moment.

You can do this by practicing a little meditation, focusing on mindfulness.

Understand motivation Why do you act in a certain way?

In order for you to understand the mind, you have to discover your motivations. One way is to play detach yourself from procrastination. You may not have that problem, but many people do, because they have so many pending tasks, more than you can imagine.

Being stuck is part of the behavior, not doing is an activity too. Before that behavior there was a feeling of motivation to do something, it could be bad like eating too much or smoking too many cigarettes or giving in to unfair demands or just things like complying with something that we previously spoke or helping a loved one.

When you analyze motivation and procrastination, go to the moment before the behavior and you will find the feeling, you can find feelings that move fast that you had not even noticed, but that get you stuck and give you anxiety about it. Then go back before the binding. Why did it happen to you?

Procrastination and its root causes How to avoid it?

The key is in the root of the procrastination, to find the image related to this. It can be difficult because the mind automates tasks. We've been doing things for years and we don't even notice when we do it anymore. It takes patience and dedication to find out what's behind this.

Follow this couple of tips:

Slower, as much as you can

For your mind when it comes to problems, let it be in slow motion. When looking for the image or voice that stops you, put everything in slow motion. Don't think about the thought, because the thought comes after the image.

Get in on doing scans and adjustments, there's no reason why you shouldn't look around, it's just a new skill. You must give yourself your time. If you examine anything you've put off, the reason you put it off may be your brain seeking to protect you.

Recognize confusion for what it really is

As you search for the root of procrastination, you may be feeling confused. This is a code, you are angry or afraid. The code protects you. Look around and you will see that there is a low feeling, which is perhaps less pleasant. Play back images in slow motion and define decision points.

You have a thought, you give it meaning and then you add emotion to it, you do the behavior, for now let's not worry about changing it. It is the wrong end of the lever. You have to work the opposite, because it is easier to manipulate the image or the trigger, since there are no attached feelings there and therefore there are no risks.

Eliminate negative auditory cues

It would be good if you listened to your inner voice. It may be that that voice discourages you from doing something, that it takes away your confidence in yourself. They are pieces from our first years of life that have generally been overcome, but the voices are still there. We never turn them off, that's why they resonate. So, go in to see what you hear and where the sound is coming from.

Make the brain hear that voice, as soon as the first sound starts, press the volume control to make it go away quickly. The next step is that somewhere you see a stranger and deduce if he is someone nice or not, that you read the message that he emanates. Now, you have to make an image of yourself, see what you say about yourself or how safe you feel.

Now you tell yourself that you feel safe, secure, protected. You say things to yourself where there is no negativity.

The next step is the sound of the waves to clean everything. You can feel it like waves hitting the sand over and over again, as soon as that ugly word comes, it just goes away and you feel safe, the waves come.

When you notice the feelings or behaviors, hit the brakes, check to see what happens. If it was an image that awakened everything, change the experience by playing with visual submodalities.

How to control your emotions with NLP: Travel passengers

Feelings are just options and there are options to make major changes. When feelings are treated as options rather than as things to be endured. You have the opportunity to make decisions and the difference it will make for you depends on the amount of time and energy you put into these skills.

As you tune in to what you feel, it will be easier to go back, and you will notice the image or sound that led to the feeling. NLP will help you address frustrations, irritations, and anxieties, if you install behind them a state of curiosity to know why you feel that way.

Curiosity helps develop new synapses. Helps strengthen the brain and generate more engagement. When you explore an answer with a stronger sense of curiosity, you see that incredibly many negative things disappear and you open the door to new possibilities.

When you feel that something frustrates you, try not to let the mind wrap you with bad thoughts, because you will fall into a loop where it will be more difficult to get out.

If you work on curiosity, it will kick your brain and give you a totally different track, and you will see how the frustration, irritation and anxiety will disappear in you. You will begin to notice how each feeling started.

Emotions are caused by a signal, this is the same although the stimulus is different because the signal carries emotion. This is like a flash, it happens very fast. The only way to do this is by slowing things down, taking deep breaths, and performing the mental action at a low speed.

Before you you have to see that person that you are, without problems, a perfect being, you have to take a moment before the cycle begins again.

To close this part, remember, find the track for emotion, destroy the signal and immediately change it with a future where you have no problems and you are curious. Do it and you will notice the profound change.

How to eliminate depression

Negative feelings are often related to auditory cues, voices in the mind. I want to give you some tips to help you deal with depression

Depression is very debilitating, it is difficult to cope with it. It is important to rethink the purpose as depression makes no sense when taking a problem or bad news and making it personal.

Depression is when a person is not in the mood for anything, and it takes it to the point of making it a habit. It is a painful way to live, if you feel depressed, if the world is against or you feel that nothing is going to work, go inside and explore to see what happens.

Remember that there is no internal enemy. If you feel bad and you do not know the reason, it is good that you assume that there are positive reasons for feeling this way, you have something inside that tries to do you good even if you are fatal.

Listen to the inner voice, if it is a voice that repeats itself, you have a couple of things to do: You dissociate yourself, ceasing to be in the image to see yourself in it. If it's a voice, let it speak from across the room.

Make the voice more seductive, it could be the voice of a child yawning, maybe it would be good to send it to sleep. The idea is that you find out what happens in the head so that the emotion occurs and then interfere with the sequence.

You can experiment with different changes in submodalities until you get some relief from heaviness, darkness, heavy silence, or what is stored within you.

BRUTAL NLP

Chapter 3

Knowing persuasion

E very technique I present in this book has been tested by experts and has been experienced by many people. What you will read below will open your mind to the true world of persuasion.

What you need to communicate successfully

Simplicity is worth gold, when you talk to others you have to do it in a simple way, so that they can understand it regardless of the academic degree they have. The world has evolved so much that many day-to-day processes have been simplified. We are in a world of instant messages, of a face or a sticker in response to a person.

If you are going to say something, you have to do it in a simple and brief way, if a sentence is enough, do not invert a paragraph. Simplicity should not be used alone, you have to apply repetition, the so-called illusion of truth, and this is because if it is repetitive it becomes familiar. When a message is received over and over again, it feels familiar. That is why politicians know how to use it because there is no great difference between the real truth and the illusion of it.

People rate repeated statements as having more validity than if they had just heard them. That is why repetition has become one of the simplest and most widely used persuasion methods.

But repetition has its flaws, it happens when people analyze repetitive arguments and notice that they have weak foundations, and there they fall. It happens daily in the scandals that are formed on the internet that are born from a message or a photo where the message is misrepresented.

Al Gore during his presidential campaign in 2000 declared that he had been the inventor of the Internet, when his job was to be the first political leader to recognize the importance of the great network. This, far from giving him credibility, made him the object of ridicule. It is even said that it affected his path to the presidency. That is why you have to keep in mind that reputation is very valuable and must be preserved because it can be lost with just a couple of lines.

I invite you to do an experiment, you can do it with your family circle, separate into two groups of 10 people, now, you ask each group a question.

Ask the first group: Shouldn't medical care be given to people without papers?

Second group question: Should medical care be denied to the undocumented?

You are going to see the impact of these words that you chose. These are questions that have been asked in various investigations and the results say that only 38% believe that medical care should be "denied", while 55% believe that medical care should not be given. Therefore the difference lies in the assumptions. "Deny" falls on the personal or social rights of a person who can lose. Now, with "giving" you something, the law is not necessarily affected, therefore the context determines the reaction of those who hear the question.

Another mistake is to assume that people have the same definition of a word, for example, today "I believe" and "I feel" are used a lot, for some it is just something linguistic, but you do have differences, barely perceptible, but there are .

If we see this: "I think the recovery of the economy is going to happen from one moment to the next" and "I feel that the recovery of the economy is going to happen from one moment to the next," they send the same message, but in research It is found that that small difference can influence the power of the persuasive message.

We build the world with feelings, unpleasant or pleasant, comforting or scary, we also build it with thoughts, such as useful or useless, beneficial or harmful, etc.

In an exercise related to what was said in the previous paragraph, a group of people were placed with their constructions of the world in particular and given a persuasive message that talked about donating blood. The message contained the same arguments, except that one message said "think" and the other said "feel." At the end, each person was asked about the chances of donating blood in the future.

Those who thought about the world cognitively were more likely to give blood when the message was framed in terms of "thinking." Those who used emotional words were more persuaded when the term "feel" was used.

This suggests that when you want to persuade someone, it is good to know if it is a person who focuses on thoughts or feelings and to direct the message accordingly.

Cialdini's Principles of Persuasion

Robert Cialdini is a must when it comes to persuasion. He is one of the great experts on issues of influence and persuasion, therefore it is important that you know his 5 principles and how to use them in others.

Principle 1: Reciprocity

When one person has a gesture with another, the person referred to feels the need to return the gesture. An example is the Hare Krishnas, who give a flower or a book and when the "gift" is accepted, they immediately ask for a donation.

When you give something to another person and they say "thank you" and you reply "It was nothing" or something similar, you are inadvertently reducing the favor they have given, therefore they feel they owe nothing. Instead, you could say, "I know you would do the same for me." You respond amiably and maintain the feeling of debt with a space for them to correspond to you.

Principle 2: Commitment and consistency

When an idea is committed, in writing or orally, the commitment is more likely to be fulfilled. Even when there is no incentive to do so or if the motivation or incentive is removed after the agreement, the reason is that the commitment is consistent with the self-image.

An experiment was conducted in the 1960s where researchers posing as volunteer workers asked owners to install a large, ugly fence on their homes that said "Drive carefully." Of course, practically no one wanted to do this, and as a result, only 17% of the owners accepted the request. Now, when they made a small adjustment, the rate went from 17 to 76%. How was it achieved? You'll see.

A couple of weeks earlier, investigators asked owners to display a small 3-inch sign that read "Be a Safe Driver." Since this request was unimportant, almost everyone agreed. However, when another volunteer returned a couple of weeks later, the owners were more receptive to putting up the larger sign. Why, when accepting to put the small notice, did they feel the need to accept to put the other large one that was so invading their property?

Out of the need to be consistent in all areas of their lives. That's why when you want to use this principle to your advantage, have one person do something small to establish the small commitment and then they will surely stay committed for bigger requests.

Principle 3: Social proof

Imagine this: you are going on a trip and in a place you see two restaurants, one full of cars and the other almost empty, which one are you going to? In 9 out of 10 people go to the full house. You are not going "despite" being full but "because" it is full. It happens that they assume that being full, the food there will be more delicious. That is social proof.

That is why you see marketing strategies where they say "Join the more than 500 thousand members already active" or similar. Therefore this is one of the most powerful persuasion methods, you can use it by showing opinions, testimonials and people who use what you teach. You can use it to create consensus, for example if almost everyone agrees with something, then the less sure are more likely to accept because it is the opinion of the majority.

Principle 4: Authority

People tend to obey authority figures, even when questionable or unethical things are asked. An example of this is the Milgran experiment. It was a group of researchers who put participants to "electrocute" actors who pretended to go through the condition. Participants were unaware that there were actually no electric shocks, just performance. The actors screamed and pleaded for him to stop, but due to the great power of authority, practically all continued to electrocute the victims who were crying out for mercy.

There was another somewhat humorous experiment, a notice was posted on an ATM that read "Out of service, turn over your deposits to the policeman." The experiment was carried out by a journalist dressed as a policeman, with a uniform, a badge, and even a baton. The journalist managed to collect $ 10,000 in cash and checks, and this in just two hours. Not counting the bank details that people gave him, from secret codes to social security numbers.

When the journalist showed who he really was, he asked people why they had given in to the request and they said because of the uniform. Keep this in mind, authority is about more than strength, it's also about appearances.

While you probably won't be dressing up as a police officer, you can show your authority with confident body language and a firm, resonant and authoritative tone of voice.

Principle 5: Taste

People tend to be more persuaded by those they like. On one occasion, a group of vendors was studied. Those who sold the most were those who created a "relationship" with customers, conversed, listened, and got to know some things about the other person's life, in contrast to those who knocked on more doors, even the latter had rather numbers negatives.

That is the power of taste. People prefer to negotiate with those they like.

These principles of influence allow you to take advantage of the basic human needs for which people take action and therefore this serves to influence and persuade.

Michael Moore knows how to use psychological techniques

Moore was the one who published Fahrenheit 9/11 in 2004, a work that dealt with his personal vision of how George Bush used the 9/11 attacks to create wars in Afghanistan and Iraq. His work was either loved or hated. Around this time, Dr. Kelton Rhoads, an expert in persuasion psychology, wrote a few techniques used by Moore in his work and it is a good introduction to propaganda techniques. Although the techniques are not directly related to language patterns, you will see how useful they can be in persuasive messages.

Omissions

It is one of the most obvious techniques. Not showing the whole truth, grants omissions that the audience does not recognize as absent. Therefore it makes people draw conclusions. Moore did not show the planes hitting the twin towers, which would have caused anger in the viewer, what he showed was the consequence of the acts, which caused pain in the viewer.

Contextualization

Here Moore uses structural activation, for example, if you feel sad at a given moment, this tends to portray what will happen next. For example, contextualization often makes Bush seem silly, in the first scene you see sad people suffering from the attack, in the next we see Bush smiling and confident, all this done on purpose so that viewers can feel what they surely feel right now. .

Group manipulations

In short, it is preferring "people like us" over "people who are not like us." An example of this is that in the documentary the Saudis are portrayed as part of the group that is with Bush and that he is with the Bin Laden family by association. Then it shows that Bin Laden is close to Osama Bin Laden, even by association. Here the only connection is the association.

Cynicism

People tend to attribute selfish motivations to others and altruistic motivations to our way of acting. We tend to be cynical about why others do what they do and it is easy to make people suspect someone's motivations just by questioning them.

An example of this is that Bush is said to act for his own interests and not for the United States, the president is shown reading in a school for children for seven minutes after the secret service whispered in his ear what happened. The assumption is that he was confused or did not care. Although there is also the possibility that the agent told him to wait to seek the best action in search of protecting him.

Modeling

People always copy themselves from others, it is their nature. If you stop on a street and look at nothing or the window of a building, in a short time you will have others by your side doing the same. If you see this in political terms, the same thing happens. If people see another change their point of view, this will influence people in the same way.

For example, in the documentary there is a mother mourning the death of her son in Iraq, which gives a 180 ° turn to the work, showing support for Bush, from supporting the war to the opposition. Everything, according to experts, manufactured to make the message that the documentary wanted to convey more persuasive.

Numerical deceptions

People like numbers, statistics. For example, it is said that Bush was on vacation 42% of the time during his first 229 days in office. This refers to the time he was out of Washington and the truth is that they say that if he is not in the White House, he does not work. It is like saying that if you are at home sitting at the computer you do not work, because you are not in an office. Everything always depends on how you see it and how you want to show the message to another.

*Chapter*4

Do you live in a comfortable place that is not so comfortable?

People spend much of their lives living in places that they feel comfortable, but are actually far from it, either because they live by expectations, resist trauma, or lack the real motivator to move forward. We are going to see in this chapter what it is about and how we can work on it.

The impact of your expectations

You may have a desire for a new job, because you feel like you can easily switch from the one you are in. Also, you may not feel like doing it, because you saw that your best friend had a hard time getting one and you do not want to go through the same or worse.

Perspectives and expectations influence us, what we decide and what we do. Expectations may be out of reach and may not even be accurate. Let's see this with an example:

Stand upright, with your feet shoulder-width apart. Put your right arm out, turn your torso gradually to the left, move your arm to the left as much as you can. Using the arm and hand that is across the body, point to the farthest one, and rotate it and see where it is.

Now come back. This exercise teaches you something, that knowledge is just hearsay unless it's in the muscle.

Now while you are still, imagine that you can rotate your right torso and arm more to the left than before, imagine what it would feel like if you could loosen your torso and shoulders so that the right arm reaches further to the left.

Extend your right arm and slowly turn it to the left, discover how far you can go now with just this change in your imagination.

Reduce resistance to trauma

Take a pencil and paper, think of something you need to do, but when you imagine that you do it, you feel your energy drop, on a scale of one to ten, where ten is more resistance, how strong is your resistance to doing this task? Just make a mental note of this.

Now take the pencil and hold it in front of your face about twelve inches away. You can see its tip, now remember the task to be done, imagine that you can put the sensation of resistance on the tip of the pencil, when this is done, put your gaze on it. Then, with the pencil you draw a figure of 8 sideways in the air, while you do it you keep your head still, only the eyes follow the tip of the pencil.

As you draw it, as you get closer to the middle, where the lines intersect, sweep up, go up, and follow the loop on the left.

Make at least 5 full loops in the shape of an 8, when you finish, see the resistance level from one to ten again. It sure has improved a lot. If you dare, you can repeat the exercise with the 8.

You can do this exercise as many times as you want, you will notice the changes almost immediately, because the brain works fast.

Enthusiasm and optimism serve as drivers

Energy, enthusiasm, and optimism are great drivers that influence how we feel. What level of optimism do you have today? You are happy? Are you thankful

Motivation is the premium of enthusiasm, for example, you have something to do, like organize your finances and you do not know how to motivate yourself to start. People can be motivated in two ways, one is by creating anxiety and the other by creating a positive experience. Both with different emotional connotations.

If you are one of those who use anxiety, you may not finish everything before the deadline and end up with problems related to non-compliance. However, some people get so anxious that they freeze and are unable to do anything.

Now if you think positive, think about how you got out of bed this morning and what you said to yourself when you woke up. What were those motivators?

Although you may not be an early riser, getting up early is possible using NLP. Achieving it is easy, every time you go to sleep think about what you want to do the next day, it can be worked, going for a walk, fulfilling a commitment ...

If you currently wake up with stressors, better not continue at that. Look for experiences based on pleasure, look for positive feelings to do it.

Increase confidence

Before tackling how you can work on trust, we have other issues to tackle. Let's start by analyzing this, people seek eternal confidence as they seek permanent happiness. If you were so confident you could do anything, like cross a highway at rush hour without looking to the sides, because you are confident that you will get to the other side unscathed. How do you see that?

There is a confidence that you always have and that you should use more, it is the ability to learn; It is that strong sense of confidence to learn in whatever situation you face that will keep your energy high.

Think of a situation where you feel very confident in your abilities, it can be anything, make breakfast, change a tire or whatever, go to the submodalities and feel what happens in that moment in you. Visualize that in the mind for you to associate. In this way you get information, you will hear the internal dialogue and you will know that you are aware of the situation.

Now think of a pending situation to address and where you doubt yourself, go in and notice the differences with what you can do easy. You must feel everything and identify where mistrust happens in your body. Make the changes for the images that you lived when you felt safe, change what you heard and what you perceived in each sense.

This is a simple exercise that you can apply every day for at least a week or two, if you want to build a more confident state of mind.

This is how Navy SEALs are motivated

One way to build trust is to work on inside knowledge just like Navy SEALs do. To begin with, they have the most difficult military training in the world, with preparation inspired by the methods used by the British Special Air Services with their commandos.

SEALs go through a six-week training where they rank the best. They call it Hell Week, it is a space where they sleep 4 hours in 70 hours. They also go through phases of very cold or humidity, at this stage they select people with high IQ and of course, great physical abilities. It happens that these people who participate in the initial six weeks, of all, only 24% remain, the rest drop out.

This was seen as a problem, so years ago they hired Eric Potterat, who is a psychologist and became a command master of the SEALs.

Potterat created a program where he works four habits and managed to increase graduation by 50%. He saw what in NLP is called "the difference that makes the difference."

All that said, let's start looking at these 4 habits that are the difference between life and death or a mission won or failed and how they can be used.

Habit one: focus on the now

The best way to deal with stress when you do something is to limit your focus. You must do it in the immediate future, the SEALs are focused on reaching the end of the twenty-mile race. They don't think of anything else, no meals, no payments, nothing, just that. You will see that you achieve better results.

Habit two: imagine how good you will feel

It is related to rehearsing past successes. When you go through win lists in partnership, when you finish with 20 or 30 of these hits, you will be familiar with the feeling in the body that shows you satisfaction with yourself.

The plan is for you to transfer the wonderful feelings to the present moment. What you do here is use the most positive submodalities. You pass it on to any area of what you do and tell yourself how good it feels to progress.

Divide the task into smaller ones so that the small achievement feels good and continue. You can do this as many times as you want so that you notice the progress you are making and you will have access to these whenever you want.

Habit three: when all else fails, take a deep breath

There comes a time when we get discouraged, lose heart, or are very exhausted. It is when that kind of collapse happens that we believe that we will not be able to advance any further.

It is there when small parts of the brain emerge that take over our life. That's where the amygdala works in the brain that tells us if something is right or not. So when you feel like you're failing, the amygdala decides that everything has gone to hell, then you go into panic or anxiety boxes.

In these situations, it is best to fill the body with oxygen, you change the blood chemistry and the amygdala.

To apply this habit, when you are in an upset emotional situation, start with this:

Inhale deeply for a count of six, hold, for a count of two, now exhale for a count of six, make sure to empty your lungs. You must do it three times and you will notice the changes immediately, your blood pressure drops, the brain fills with oxygen and the ability to think increases. This way you react more positively.

Habit Four: Cheer Up

This has to do with the voices we hear in our minds. SEALs are taught to be their own cheers for encouragement. They have a voice that tells them that if they made a mistake, forget the mistake and move on.

Instead of whipping each other for what happened, they cheer up and reassure themselves that they will succeed in winning the mission, no matter if they have a blister on their foot, the backpack is broken, they have no water or they shoot at all fronts.

It is a methodology that works for people who are in challenging situations.

The next time you go through anxiety situations and feel a little scared, think about applying your breath and each of the SEAL habits to increase your confidence and motivation.

How to silence your negative inner voice

I have already told you about the voices in your mind, your own and those of others that were important to us and sometimes resonate within us when we are faced with a certain situation. Just as SEALs have positive voices that encourage you to continue, we tend to be negative about some situations and take it upon ourselves to say harmful phrases that increase demotivation.

Voices steal fun out of life and the energy you have is gone, as well as the will to succeed. When you go through this, what you can do is:

First you set a trap, you are attentive, as soon as it begins and you feel a negative message, you eliminate it before it takes on size, you change the thought for a positive one. When you notice it, you have options, you let the critical voice give you the options and little by little you work to change the tonality from dark to something fun, that is, you play with the submodalities.

Apply what you want, you can put a comic voice, a cartoon, or whoever you want, you will notice that when you do it, the critical voice stops and with it the feelings about what you do.

Chapter5

Learn to better connect with others

I have talked about how the brain works and how you can make changes to make everything work better, everything you learned happens inside of you. It also happens within other people, we all have the same experience structure, we receive stimuli, you can call them memories or something external. Then the brain assigns a meaning to it and triggers emotions and these a behavior.

Let's learn how to establish connections with others starting from our own connection and the way in which we interact.

Internal representational systems, do we all process information the same?

Everything you have learned in this book happened within you, as well as you, others have lived the experience with the content, although for each one it is perceived differently.

For example, in your case, some types of stimuli appeared, a memory or something that comes from the outside, then the brain gives it meaning and triggered emotions.

What do we have to do in ourselves before dealing with others? To achieve this you have to seek to be aware of what you think. Wonderful people emphasize testing their thinking, this makes them bypass the mental and personal filters. This way you get the real information as it arrives. People who do this effectively can connect well with one another, as they are considered good company and are enjoyed being with.

How the three parts of your brain work

If you have analyzed what happened in the past, you know what behaviors or ways of being have to improve. Everything that you are radiates in others and in the state of mind that you project. This has its reason, it happens that the brain has different parts and functions.

In studies it has been discovered that in the interaction there is a slower conscious reason and the instinct and emotion is faster. The architecture of the brain ensures that we feel first and then think. The part of the brain where instinctive fight or flight signals are activated first, the amygdala, is positioned in such a way that it receives incoming stimulus before the thinking parts of the brain.

This part of the brain is usually activated when we meet someone, it is as if they said "pay attention, look around, confirm that everything is fine." It is usually turned off when confirming that everything is okay, but sometimes the amygdala yells at you to run or fight.

It also happens when we talk with another person, we want to go from feeling to thinking to be able to speak. Now that we touch on this point, I want to take the opportunity to talk to you about the positions, this is part of the submodalities, and it serves to better interact with other people.

The first position is about your own body, you see everything through your eyes, you know how you feel, what you want and it is a position of great authenticity. In NLP it is the position of the self.

The second position is that where you are very nice, you feel what the other suffers, it is where the other is understood. In this position, if we go too far we can be too demanding and over-dependent. This position is called Others.

In NLP, the third position is called the Observer, it is where you are out of the situation and see what happens. You are separate from yourself. It is a position widely used by scientists, surgeons, engineers and other professionals. They are people who go out of themselves to judge what happens.

These positions serve to gain clarity about what is going on inside and outside in a given situation.

In these societies they encourage us to get out of the first position, girls should not be selfish, boys should not cry, it is not male, in sports it is invited not to take it personally even if it is exciting, in the mafia the previous murderer to shoot says they are just business.

Second position is a good place to dwell when we meet others, but not to stay there. You only go to get information and then leave. Live more in first position to get clarity about how you feel and go to the other two.

Adjust and balance your inner world so that you are better company

You choose to be who you are, your thoughts, feelings and actions. Also, the way you reconfigure yourself is an option, you can rewire your brain, just like when you choose to remodel the house.

Let's go back to interacting with others, imagine a virtual mirror where you can see images of how you look, sound and behave when you are with others. What do you like more? Maybe you are a good listener, you bring a lot of energy and laughter to the meeting, you are wise and interesting. What makes you good company?

Think of that moment where you felt good after a conversation and what you did to be like that. When you have done this, you look at yourself again and analyze what you can do to be better with others and with yourself.

Maybe in the process you will find moments where you are not proud of yourself, the good thing is that this has already happened and you have in your hands the option not to do it, to control your future behaviors.

If you want to change for the better, you can ask yours if they help you improve some aspects to be able to connect better with others. You can ask him:

- What do you like the most when we interact or spend time together?

When they tell you what they think, make sure you understand the message and go to the other question:

- If I could change one thing about how I interact with you, what would it be?

You may not like the answer I give you very much, but do not take it personally, remember that it is part of your improvement process. By overcoming this question you can go to the last one:

- What would you like me to start doing?

With these answers you will be able to know what makes you good company and what aspects you can improve to be it, maybe there are actions that you did not know that caused itching in others and just by stopping doing it, you would greatly improve your relationship with them.

Not everything is mirroring to establish and generate connections

From the second position is that the other is mirrored, although that is not all, you also have to take care of the content and the quality of the conversations, because these determine whether or not the bodies coincide with each other.

The difference between mirroring and imitating is a fine line that could make others suspicious. If someone feels that you imitate him, he will create dissonance, he will think "this one does everything I do, what happens to him?"

The idea at this point is that the mirroring is done, looking for similarity in the tone of voice, that is, keeping the same tone, not higher or lower, achieving the imitation in a subtle way, not immediately after the other makes the voice. movement, always considering how the person feels, the culture they have, you also have to bear in mind that you should not be on top of the person, but keep a certain distance, one where you touch them by stretching your hand, a way of having some intimacy, but without occupying the other's personal space.

How to help others feel more secure

Here are three easy ways to make others feel safe:

With a glance, eye contact, is a way of helping him feel cared for. A look can be very attractive, as adults when we feel flirtatious and want to make a romantic connection with someone, we can observe the other person a little longer.

When you are chatting with a person, you can look them in the eye and then look away slightly, then make eye contact again. In this way, the person will not feel intimidated, but you will be attentive and listen to them. This leaves good results for the other.

A quick exercise, go directly into the eyes of people you don't usually do, such as the waiter, the toll booth or the one who stamps your parking ticket, this makes you recognize them as individuals, when you say thank you or say please can you look them in the eye. You will see how relationships and treatment with you improve.

Another way to make the other feel good is that we synchronize with their body language, allow your attention to rest on them. Talk to them, being interested in their topics, if they tell you something, you can ask them more about it, questions that are not so invasive or according to the level of trust they have, but that show that you have an interest in listening to them.

The plan in this part is to try to make a good first impression, you must make sure that the other person feels good. Keep in mind that that first impression is 50% internal work, it is managing yourself so that the other person feels safe and the other 50% is managing the conversation so that the other feels interesting.

When you ask them how they feel and you touch a nerve, the emotional side appears there, then you can show that you are very interested in what happens in them, you share the feeling, perhaps the frustration of a certain situation, the pain, the joy or the emotion you have with that situation.

People are not always used to someone caring about how they feel and less talking about it, but we can explore those things in a way that feels safe and validated, the idea is to show that you care more about how they feel than about make them feel a certain way.

As we gain this kind of internal influence and get the job done, we end up being a better company that allows us to have more pleasant interactions and relationships.

*Chapter*6

Working the language of people

Now that you have been getting to know all these NLP tools, you can apply them to be able to start influencing other people and get them to think the way you want. Let's see how to do it in this chapter.

The power of reasons and suggestions

Harvard University psychologist Ellen Langer did a surprising experiment, she was in line to get some photocopies and she said to the one in front of her: "Excuse me, I have 5 pages, can I use the machine?" this with the intention of getting ahead of those who were ahead.

He found that 60% of people allowed them to pass by, so Langer was clearer: "Can I get these copies? I'm in a hurry" by giving a reason the rate increased to 94% acceptance.

He tried again, this time he said "I have five pages, can I use the machine, because I have to make some copies" the rate stayed almost the same as it barely dropped 1%. By using the word "because" he achieved that result.

If we think about the reason, surely you were or had a child "because" who was that child who to everything they said, responded with a "why?" it is a natural part of the children's process. It is the moment when the left hemisphere of the brain connects and the concept of cause and effect is forming.

The brain begins to feel that it knows the cause of every effect it sees. There is something key in this, the brain only wants to feel the cause even if it does not understand it. If we analyze Langer's research, we find a small drop when the motive is eliminated, we must recognize this: as the objective increases in complexity, the reason or why it must also be increased, that is why it has an almost magical effect on decisions fast. So, the why placed in a petition works because it responds to the constant why of the people.

Now let's talk about the five types of needs that all human beings seek to satisfy and that Abraham Maslow talks about.

If you want to motivate someone to do any meaningful action, give them a why, followed by these 5 needs, you will create a lot of motivation. These are the 5 needs:

3. Physiological needs
4. Security
5. Belonging
6. Recognition
7. Self realisation

Now we are going to give a little twist to the matter to find six basic motivators:

I need it, I have to, I want, I choose, I love it, it is a calling.

Let's delve into this, imagine that you ask a man who goes with a briefcase very early, why is he going to work, he will tell you that because he has to pay bills and that if he does not work he does not eat, this is a necessity, it is part of the many people who go to work out of necessity and hate that job and seek daily loopholes.

Now you go and ask another the same and he answers that he has to put a roof over the head of the family, pay for insurance, give them everything they need. He is a person who acts with whom I have to do it, he has a little more motivation than the previous one, his family is his engine.

You go and ask another and he says that he goes because he likes it, that he is not like his colleagues who hate work, he likes his team, he likes his work and he loves to be active. This is a person who goes to work because he wants to, he has a little more motivation than the previous ones.

Now you ask another and he tells you that they just called him, that it was supposed to be his day off, but that there is a lot of fuss, well, it does not bother him, also this act of the day will make him look good in the annual performance evaluation . This is a person who chooses to work and has more motivation than all the previous ones, although that motivation may be a bit self-centered, it is a person who could sabotage others to achieve a better position.

Given the above, I will now talk about those that concern us, if you want to motivate or inspire someone you have to find a reason for their brain to feel good. Now, when you ask someone what motivates them, don't do it directly, you can for example say "Why did you choose this profession?" there you will find what really drives them. The rest is to touch the specific emotional keys to come up with the suggestion of what you want them to think.

I will explain a bit to put you in context, if I tell you to think at this moment in simple geometric figures, such as a square and the like, surely you think of a circle or a triangle. It is not that I am a fortune teller, but that I know that the brain takes shortcuts, it does not want to work more than necessary, it seeks simple answers.

When I say to you, "in this moment" I create the sense of urgency. When I say "simple" I eliminate a large number of possible options and remove more complex figures like a dodecagon from the game. Also, I removed the square option because I used it as an example when I invited you to think of a simple geometric figure. You stop thinking about my suggestion and create yours which is circle or triangle.

So persuading is not cajoling, it is leading. If you feel that they pressure you to do something, you put the shields, there the "why" disappears, even if you put a great reason, the other person will reject it no matter what they are told. So instead of giving someone a thousand reasons for something, ask why? So that you find the "why".

An example, you ask your child: Why should we treat adults with respect? This engages the listener in what they just heard and feels like it was their idea.

The word because it is powerful, the reason is that it satisfies the need for cause and effect in the brain. You see that sometimes it is better to ask "why?" to say "why".

How to be a persuasion expert

Nobody wants to be persuaded or manipulated, there is something called free will that people respect a lot, so we have some resistance tricks to defend ourselves against those persuasions. That's why we resist a lot of the advertisements and all the calls-to-action messages that we don't obey.

In an experiment where they had a group of people and they were asked to choose between two similar soccer teams, one of the participants who was actually an actor, said "You definitely have to choose team X", 76.5% chose the rival team. That is reverse psychology acting.

Eric Knowles and Jay Linn published the book Resistance and Persuasion, where they talk about four barriers of psychological resistance that oppose persuasion, we are going to see it with an example so that you understand it better.

Someone tries to sell you life insurance, it is the best, it is perfect for you, but you are a difficult customer to convince. The salesperson says to you "Have you considered having life insurance? I think this policy is perfect for you ". There he applied the hard sale, there came your first barrier and you tell him not to try to sell an insurance that you do not need. It happens that when you recognized that they wanted to sell you something, you put your defenses up, this is called the "reactance" barrier, there you put yourself in your thirteen and the game is over.

Now, if the seller had used the "yes" I would have had better luck, something like "If someone in the same situation came to me, I would recommend policy X" the comment sounds innocent and even sweet, such a concerned seller.

The seller does not recommend anything, it is for someone else and the "yes" opens the gap to what you think, the resistance weakens.

But you are a tough customer, the barrier of "mistrust" appears and you tell him that he commented on that because he is alone after his commission. That he is one more scammer.

Then, the seller responds that "yes, there are definitely scam sellers, I have suffered them. But, even if the cure for cancer appears, we should first sell the idea, is that scamming? No, now, this policy does not cure cancer, but what if this is the cure for your life insurance problem? " With this the seller passes this barrier, but you are a tough bone and you continue.

Then you object for the price or any other excuse, it is the third barrier, that of "scrutiny", it is where you weigh pros and cons and it is a peak moment where the sale can fall. But the "yes" again helps.

"If I could show you how to have the benefits of this policy at a very affordable price, would you do it?" Is the seller's heavy weapon. If you decide that you are committed, if you say no, you disagree with yourself, and now we are facing a stronger resistance, "inertia", which to break it has to break behavior patterns, which is very hard on people.

Inertia is the gap between saying we will do something and actually doing it. Maybe you feel that the policy suits you, but you can't make up your mind, you say you'll think about it for a few days. The "yes" comes back to play and the seller says:

"In a few days many things can happen, what would happen to your family, if, God forbid, something will happen to them between now and a few days? How would you feel having postponed this? "

There the anticipation of regret has been applied. In studies when phrases like "you definitely have to choose such a thing" are used and they put the "you will regret if later you win" something like "You definitely have to buy Bitcoins because they will go from 7 thousand dollars to 60 thousand and you will regret if you do not invest now same".

The anticipation of repentance totally changes the behavior of the person and they act out of that fear of not repentance later.

In other circumstances they can use the phrase with the "yes": "I'm not sure if this is for you, but ...", it is a phrase that does not have pressure, because you suggest that the listener is not interested, but you increase the intrigue and interest, you also put the word "but" that also has strength in the persuasion process. The word "but" denies all of the above, you make the voice of the listener say "that may interest me" and pay attention to see if they are interested or not.

How to alter the status of others

What is the reason for changing the emotional state of another? Each belief, decision and thought has emotionality, sometimes this is big, but other times it is so small that it is not even known if we want it to be present. Emotion is in everything we do and plays a key role in decisions.

What you decided when you were angry, sad or happy, is different than if you had decided with another state of mind. So if we change the emotion, we change the belief.

For example, if I told you now, "When I really have a good idea, I start to feel like my stomach is tingling up my chest as I think about all I can do with the new concept. This is how you know you have a good idea. " If you noticed it there, I gave you instructions on how to feel like a good idea, I started talking about me and ended up talking about you. People hardly perceive this.

If I say "I want you to be curious" you will have an internal representation to understand what I am saying, although you do not have to connect these elements, so a sentence will have a lot of effect on you. But if I said "when I feel curious, I feel a kind of buzzing in my head and an attraction to the subject, as if it were a magnet that does not let me escape until I learn more" I give you instructions on how to be curious and make a change in the index referential. In this situation your brain will want to answer the question and to do so it has to try both sentences and compare results, so the words would be causing access to the feelings.

To find a person's feelings you have to:
- Give internal presentations directly.
- Offer a process for feelings.
- Ask questions.

Using the combination of the previous three can give phrases like this "I don't know if you will find this interesting, of course, when I came across these concepts, I suddenly started thinking about many applications and I went from interest to ecstasy as I went through all of them. I felt a rise in temperature in my chest as more ideas appeared. How do you know when you go from interest to ecstasy?

With the above, you then know how to access people's emotions, now let's see a language pattern that will allow people to get emotionally involved with what you say.

We already know that people decide by emotion, then use reason and logic to justify their decisions. There is a pattern of NLP that takes advantage of this, it is easily used, saying things like "think how much happiness you will feel when you finish painting that picture."

Think about the type of emotion you would like the person to feel, and then think about how the person can achieve the results they want by doing what you want them to do. Something like "Think how envious they will be when you ride that motorcycle."

No matter what you think you sell, in the end you sell emotions and feelings. People buy this and justify it with decisions of logic and reason. They all seek benefits such as:

- Earn money.
- Save money and time.
- Feel safe.
- Improve health.
- Be more attractive.
- Look younger.
- Have good sex.
- Belong to something.
- Help the family.

If you sell something ask yourself why they would buy it. By knowing him, you will be able to access his feelings and manipulate them.

In case you want to generate emotional states, you have to work on the future projection with an embedded command and a presupposition.

You may not measure it right now, but it is a very powerful combination, the pattern is this:

"You go to [X] when I tell or show you"

You put the embedded command after "you're going to" and it is part of the emotional state. Let's see an example for you to understand:

"You will be delighted when I show you the price of this insurance policy."

"You will go crazy when I tell you what he did ..."

This motivates people to take action once emotions are triggered, especially when they are strong.

Reprogram people's minds

This is a technique used by ad writers to cause readers to change their minds about what they want. It is used to sow ideas in the minds.

The pattern is simple: "Is it (X)?" It can be something positive or not that you want people to think or believe.

Here's an example: "Are Dobermans the best house keepers?"

"Are Dobermans the most dangerous dogs in the world?"

It is a question that has a presupposition and more so when the person may not have knowledge of the subject.

The interesting thing about this is that it does not matter what people's response is, they can say yes or no, but the idea has been put in their minds and you can use it as a test element of your messages, even if they are not tests per se. .

Now, you have to think about the applications for this pattern in your life. Let's see in the next section how to influence the decisions of others.

How to influence the decisions of others?

This is known as redefining, it is used to take the conversation from one topic to another, when you talk to a person who is stuck at a point and you want them to change the subject to talk about what interests you.

This is the pattern you are going to use:

"That's not the topic, but ..." and then ask something to change the focus to what interests you. An example of this could be: "The issue is not what this author's new books cost, but how books come out every day that cover each other, what can we do to make marketing work better and sell books?"

The nice thing about this pattern is that you don't have to think hard to change the conversation. If you propose, you can use the pattern as many times as you want and without the other person feeling that you modified the topics, they will simply feel that it "flowed".

BRUTAL NLP

Chapter 7

Connect with others without affecting your essence

After having covered so many NLP theory and techniques, it is time for you to know how to apply them without the result affecting your essence and for you to know, for example, how to agree with others without your opinion varying.

How to agree with others without changing your mind

This is an incredible pattern, because it establishes a framework of agreement, even when there isn't one. It serves to lower the defenses of your interlocutor and the person to listen to you. With this, you can implement conditions depending on the harmony you achieve with the other person.

The pattern is like this: "I agree and would add", this is an example: "I agree that driving lessons are expensive and that is why everyone who takes them leaves driving like the best drivers."

Take a look at this one: "I agree that the driving course is expensive, but I would add that the important thing is not the cost per se, but that you will drive like the best.

Let's see one where someone told you something that you dislike, you can respond with "I agree with what you say ... I would add that only a complete idiot would say something like that" why not say idiot without so much thought? The idea is not what you say but what the other feels, here we want the person to feel like an idiot, but if you attack him directly saying that you do not agree, he will not listen to you and he will defend himself, but if you start with a frame in agreement the subconscious defenses will go down.

Also keep in mind these key elements that make the pattern work correctly, these elements are the words "but" and "and", see this example: "I agree, but I would add that ..." and "I agree and I would add that" If you realize it, the first sentence has the but that is a negation of the above and has less power, while the second has more impact.

How to persuade without anyone feeling manipulated?

Nobody likes to be manipulated even though we all want to influence others to some degree. How can we achieve this goal effectively? Ericksonian hypnosis has a pattern called Double bind, they are phrases that offer two or more choices, but are actually the same, let's see it in an example:

"You can go into a deep trance, right now or in a few minutes ..."

There is also the well-known "but you are free to choose."

Many psychological studies claim that this technique increases the possibility that the person will say yes.

You just have to make the request and then leave in the air the phrase that the person can reject if they wish:

"But you are free not to accept"

It is a technique that has better results face to face, although it can also be used by other means. The best thing about this pattern is that it allows you to appear unbiased by suggesting options that suit you, the pattern looks like this:

"As I see it, you have X options."

You are showing the options you have, you have the opportunity to show them in a way that favors the preferred choice. You start out by making a statement to set the scene in favor that highlights the option you are proposing. Something like that:

"So, currently you continue with that relationship that you hate, you don't enjoy anything, constant fights, they never come out and the details are gone, it's not what you want for yourself. I have shown you an opportunity that I know is what you like, you have three options, first, you could leave that relationship, be left with no one, but relieved and wait for the right person to arrive and maybe between all the waiting it turns out that it is not like you expect it.

Second, you could do nothing, you are where you are now, accept what you have and let this opportunity slip away. Or, thirdly, you could try my proposal, give it a try and see how far you can go. Of these options, which one is more convenient for you? "

End with the question so that the person feels they have to choose an option, you inflicted pain by staying where they were, you showed how difficult it would be to be looking for a new person, and you expanded your options to the point that it seems like the easiest way of all.

Now let's talk about the decoy effect that describes a situation where you have three different choices, two are legitimate and one is worse in almost all scenarios, it is just a decoy.

Let's look at this example:

- First option: Subscription to the web newsletter for 59 euros per year.
- Second option: Subscription on paper for 125 euros per year.
- Third option: Print and web subscription for 125 euros per year.

Here the lure is option two, nobody would choose it because for the same price it has three. In one experiment, three similar options were given to a group of 100 students, and the result was as follows:

- 16 students chose option 1.
- 0 students chose option 2.
- 84 students chose option 3.

Since no one chose both, what would happen if it were removed from the options? Let's see the results:

- 68 chose option 1.
- 32 chose option 3.

A big difference. By eliminating the lure, the best option speaking in money, was reduced, that is, the profit would be less for those who offer the newsletter.

So if you present different options to customers or anyone you want to influence, you can add a decoy option to highlight the option that is most convenient.

Pattern disruption and its psychological effect

This is a little known persuasion technique called "Interrupt, then restate", it is very effective and I would like you to know about it. Although this technique may seem like a simple cheap trick on the surface, it is actually very effective. Before I show it to you, I must warn you that it could be considered morally questionable.

In a study, they tested a technique that consisted of selling greeting cards, door to door, the subject was a charity, they had two strategies to sell them:

Strategy 1: In this condition people were told that it was priced at $ 3 for 8 cards. Thus they sold in 40% of the houses.

Strategy 2: With the technique that concerns us, they told people that the price was 300 cents for every 8 cards, and then they added that it was a bargain, thus they managed to get 80% of households to buy the cards.

It is just applying a small change in the words, it interrupts the routine thought processes. As people try to process the "300 cents" someone said instead of speaking in dollars. Then the "it's a bargain" is added and people are distracted. That interruption only works for a second, so staking must be done immediately before the person's judgment kicks in and considers the interruption.

The technique has been tested in many studies and has had similar results, so its effectiveness is proven. There are many simple disruptive manipulations that can confuse you. For example, if one day a car salesman tells you "New car, new woman" and immediately says something like "between you and me, this car is incredible", allow yourself a moment before deciding since this type of manipulation simple has a great power of momentary confusion.

Identity congruence as a tool to accept your suggestions

It is a technique known as the use of compound suggestions and is based on the principle of consistency whereby a person has inertia to make choices that are consistent with their identity, or in other words, that we will do our best to maintain a self-image. consistent. In this regard, research shows that once a suggestion has been accepted by the subconscious mind, it becomes easier for additional suggestions to be accepted as well.

The process is simple, you just have to say something with a high probability that the other person agrees and you give them suggestions that they want to implement, this is the structure:

"You are very well in that chair, it would be good to go into a deep trance."

"Knowing how to communicate effectively is vital to doing business, right? Your company needs this course so that it is prepared for the hard times ".

"To succeed in any area of life, it is good to have the power of influence with which to persuade people, for this it is important to have a specific method to do so. Here you will find a specific method to do it ".

It is a simple language pattern to use and it works well.

Establish successful agreements How to win the yes of others?

Sometimes to get a person to change their mind, you just need a leverage. This is a "modal operator of possibility", I will tell you in this section how it works:

"If I did X, would you be willing to listen?"

What you ask of the person can be anything from guessing a number to identifying which song is on the radio. It does not matter, the idea is to know that the other accepts an agreement and is willing to change.

Another technique is known as "foot in the door," and it causes a person to accept a large request by asking for a small request first. It works thanks to the principle of consistency, let's see it with an example called The cookie and the mouse:

Once upon a time, a boy gave a cookie to a mouse. He asked for a glass of milk, then the mouse wanted a straw to drink the milk. As he wanted to avoid the mark of a milk mustache, the mouse asked for a mirror, now looking at his reflection he decided to cut his hair and asked for a pair of scissors, then to sweep up the hair residue, he asked for a broom, as after all this feeling a bit tired, asked to read a story, take a nap, draw a picture and put it in the fridge.

When he saw the refrigerator, he became thirsty and asked for milk, repeating everything again.

Another technique is called "door in the face" and consists of asking for a large request that will surely be rejected like a salesperson. In one study the technique was investigated and participants were divided into two groups, the first one asked to spend two hours a week counseling juvenile offenders for two years, this was the big request. When they turned it down, they were asked to accompany juvenile offenders on a trip to the zoo for a day. This was the little request.

Participants in the second group only received the small request and these were the results of both experiments:

50% of the participants in the first group agreed with the small request, compared to only 17% in the second group.

The technique is based on the natural tendency to rely a lot on the first information that we find when we make decisions. When we talk about persuasion we call it an "anchor".

Imagine that you enter a musical instrument store looking for a guitar, then you see one that is similar to the one you are looking for and costs 2,000 euros. When the seller tries to sell you a guitar that costs 800 euros, it will seem like a good price, even if it is a higher price than it actually costs. In this way, the anchor has been implanted that will act as a basis for comparing everything, now it is much easier to accept a price that is still expensive, but lower than the initial price, simply because of the impression that it is cheaper.

Other patterns of language to persuade and influence others

There is no single magic pattern that will give you results immediately and that works the way you want, you have to have a series of them that will lead you to the desired results. You always have an arsenal of language patterns that you can naturally use in conversations.

We've looked at a number of patterns separately, but now we'll start putting pieces together for you to create the persuasive pattern sequences. The plan is that you can think strategically about persuasion and how to influence without having to worry about specific language patterns.

Imagine then that you are writing an essay to sell a course that you have just created and you already have several people to whom you have told the benefits of taking it, but you have not achieved the desired effect, what is there to do now? Let's see this sequence:

- Generate interest / anticipation.
- Recognize your needs.
- Establish benefits when meeting needs, which includes the vision of a future with more benefits.
- Enthusiasm to satisfy the needs, take note that it is not a process as such, it is a way of thinking about the emotional journey that the person will make.

Let's put details to understand it better.

Make a short account of the other person that has incredible results. Focus only on the result, not the way it was achieved and end with a phrase like "what would you like to achieve?"

Ask presupposing questions about what's holding the person back from achieving that goal and the implications of staying in the same situation.

Say forward-thinking phrases that relate to having the tools to do things differently and how you can improve the situation.

Associate the feelings with the product or idea that you present.

Now comes the step of processing it, think of a particular situation where you want to convince someone to do or buy something, remember that the only way to internalize and capture new information is by applying real cases.

Watch this:

"Did you meet Valeria? She managed to fulfill her dream of going backpacking to take amazing pictures in many places around the world. Now a sports brand sponsors his trips, a fortnight ago he was in India. It is incredible that the tool she needs is to think about her dreams and then materialize them ".

"Wouldn't it be amazing if you could achieve those dreams that you have? If you could do it, what dream would you make come true? What is important here in relation to...? "

Maybe you have thought about it, but since you were young you have had all those dreams and as you have grown up you are still not on your way to getting what you want. What is stopping you at this moment from going after your dreams?

Here you put your finger on the wound, increasing negative feelings about unfulfilled dreams, although this should be done carefully and not going so deep so as not to intensify the pain too much. Something smooth would be:

"Valeria's mission was to make a small change in her way of thinking and she began to materialize everything, leaving past fears and mistakes behind. You can change those beliefs too and do what you've always wanted ".

Changing from Valeria to "you" makes the emotional charge of the sentence impact in a more direct way on the other person's subconscious, since even though he knows that we are talking about Valeria, that "you" implies that he is our interlocutor whom we are addressing, but the person will not notice. Now comes another lunge:

"How would you feel if you could let go of your past and embrace the future so that you could do all that you've always dreamed of?"

There is that you put the emphasis you want and you can do it through questions where the person sees himself achieving all that you propose:

"Although the theme here is not Valeria achieving all this, it is you who can learn to do it. Would you like to know what Valeria obtained and with what could change her life forever? "

As you can see, it is not a sales script, it is just an emotional journey that you can apply as you want, and in the circumstances you have. It is up to you to think about the process and practice it mentally.

The idea is to think in terms of sequences and internal representations and how persuasive language fits perfectly and thus we will learn to have persuasive conversations without it appearing.

BRUTAL NLP

Chapter8

What determines that something is real in the minds of others?

A mong other factors, non-verbal language is almost the most important one, which shows us much of what we want to communicate and represents what is real and what is not. In this last chapter we will address this.

The non-verbal language of others gives us direction

Many books have been written on nonverbal language because of its implications and need for in-depth study. Non-verbal communication can come from a current inner state or from habits.

Take, for example, in the United States most people are comfortable with at least three feet apart, but no more than five. This space also includes how much of the person is towards the other.

We also have the posture, which is when a person is open or closed, with the chest open, uncovered; gestures are more frequently made with the hands and have culturally accepted meanings. The thumb up is a gesture of "Good work" or that you agree on something.

Now, touching a person's hand is different from hitting them roughly on the chest. The gentle touch releases oxytocin, the effect is powerful and is a topic of interesting research.

The teacher who claps the student discovers that they are more likely to perform in class. Regarding facial expressions, happiness, sadness, fear, disgust and surprise are universal expressions. A genuine smile is distinguished from one that is not, the person's eyes also become brighter. A person who is startled is likely to raise his eyebrows, his eyes will widen, and his mouth will open.

In the physiological response, there is redness, paleness, the nostrils open, the eyes water, and the chin trembles; rhythm and locomotion refer to the style of the physical moment, crawling or staggering is different from rushing or moving fast.

According to para-language experts, laughing, pausing, hesitating, talking a lot, interrupting or talking about someone gives messages, even silence says a lot.

Again, we want to focus on what we can objectively observe about non-verbal behavior, not on assigning
meanings that can only be applied to a generality rather than a specific person or context. As you can see, there is a range and a richness to non-verbal communication.

Tips for understanding the minds of others

There are people who ask questions in a way that they feel questioned or in a way that makes others feel foolish because they should have been more specific. When they speak honestly, you realize that asking and talking helps you get to know them better.

We are all very different, if you delve into this you will see that there is a lot of fabric to cut. Let's see these tips to keep in mind to better understand others.

Getting closer

It is to focus on the behavior of others instead of their feelings, this allows you to have better options and better understand their reality, so that the other person feels more understood.

Walk away

You can put yourself in the second and third position to get a better perspective. You may at times meet people with whom you feel there is more personal connection, who interact in a different way than others.

If you feel comfortable you can stay where you are, if not, you can send subtle signals to back off. In the case of comments, when you hear something you don't like, you walk away and dissociate yourself from the comment.

Speed down

Beware of the yellow lights of incongruity, each person has their internal realities, we are human, and we are not consistent. There is ambivalence in each of us.

When a person is incongruous, we see the light flashing yellow, we see something wrong, we slow down and contemplate, people notice the incongruity in us and you want to see theirs.

Imagine this, you meet someone you know at a party and they look out of place, they say "oh, how good to see you" but they have their eyes elsewhere, they seem to be moving away from you.

How would you feel in this situation? You would think that maybe he did not want to see you, he would rather talk to someone else or that something is wrong with you.

Maybe you ask him "Is everything okay? Is something happening between us? " Maybe he'll answer you "No, nothing, everything is fine, my girlfriend said she would come on time and she still hasn't arrived, I'm pissed off with her, it's my birthday, I should be here by now."

You may notice that a person says one thing, but their body language another, it may be that they have an internal conflict.

Discovering this type of incongruity is key to establishing or maintaining a good relationship and gathering information. Whenever you notice inconsistency or evidence of conflict, slow down and be cautious. Maybe what happens to that person has nothing to do with you, remember that everyone has their own troubles and you can find it at a bad time.

The power of questions

When a person tells something, their verbal description will be incomplete. People consciously delete information. In NLP the metamodel is a way of recovering information that is missing when asked to complete it. Let's see these gaps with examples:

If someone says, "I had a terrible time at that meeting," go inside and see what you get. If it is confusing you will immediately know that you need more information such as who, what, where, when, how, why. There are many details that you do not have.

The clues are taken from unspecified nouns and verbs, the missing pieces of the puzzle. Sometimes, despite body language, when you ask someone what happened directly to them, it can seem like you are challenging them. To avoid this and soften the questions you can mask them with:

"Could you tell me...?"

"I'm curious to know ..."

Sometimes people can use Nominalizations, which are an undefined abstraction. One way to recognize a nominalization is to ask:

"Can I put it on a cart?" it's a pretty abstract message. If a person says, "This is another day full of frustration," you can say, "Oh who's frustrated?"

The person will tell you: "I am frustrated!" and then you say "What made you frustrated?"

"I worked all week to deliver the work and now the client won't see it until Monday, so he won't pay me."

Now you understand the frustration of that person a little more, the idea is not to understand too quickly, it is to invest the necessary time to understand what affects the other.

Our beliefs design our experience of reality. How to identify them in others?

Sometimes people make unconscious statements, they present it as fact. On one occasion a man said:

"Time will slip from our hands if we do not act in this way ...".

This showed her inner world. Although the statement was not accurate, it did let us know how concerned he was about what would happen if we did not act quickly. That was his belief.

If you look at the ideas you can see the inner world, you can hear yourself things like "you know, every time I get a project it's a disaster that I can't finish on time".

In our internal dialogue we state things as facts, but they are not. If you listen to a belief, go inside yourself and think if that is true.

You may hear a teenager say:

"Well, I can't wear those old man's shoes with these clothes."

You can ask:

"Seriously? Why not?" and maybe he will answer you:

"Look at these shoes, this old man's color, I can't put them on, because the beige color is old man's."

There you discover beliefs of this young man and it will even seem funny, that belief like many others.

Language reveals the personal preferences of others

Belief statements are a reflection of what people prefer. A person's language will also reveal their preferred representational systems, their key metaprograms, and how they operate in relation to time. Knowing how to notice these differences prepares you to modify yours.

How would you know the preferences of the representation system of another? Imagine that when you talk to someone they say their vacation plans, they tell you that they are going on vacation in July, that they have reservations and save money, that they will return to the Caribbean to bask in the sun.

So you say, "Oh, you've already gone there, when you think about that place, what excites you?" the person is going to tell you many things, you can choose one and ask "What do you like most about that?" or something similar and they might answer:

"The colors of the Caribbean Sea, the tropical sun, the costumes of the people ..."

He will surely tell you kinesthetic descriptions and will tell you everything he feels about this place, his feelings and feelings. People describe situations with the three internal representation channels, but we always prefer one over the others. We will be more inclined towards feeling something in particular through emotional words, or through auditory words, or through mental vision of that situation.

Knowing this will allow you to get to know the person better and their preferences. Since metaprograms are unconscious and personal, they can be a source of conflict between loved ones and close ones, since they are now on your radar and you will look to them to ask how they influence interactions.

There is a metaprogram called "content". It recognizes the importance assigned to the five basic elements called "Domains" of life: people, information, things, activities and location.

With attention and practice you will notice how conversations reveal these elements, we all do them unconsciously and classify them.

As you become more aware of metaprograms, you will notice how commonalities can be a source of comfort and connection and are a source of curiosity and conflict. There is nothing right or wrong in this, everything is preference, fortunately things are not just black and white.

The psychologist and writer Allen Bluedorn, when doing research on time, found that in communication, especially non-verbal communication, there are actually two divisions of time: Monochronic and polychronic.

Monochrome time is linear. To understand it, in Germany, Canada, Switzerland, Scandinavia and in general in most of Europe and in the United States people are very linear, they are of schedules, they go at the agreed time for an appointment because that is what matters, they say that time is money and that it will never return.

Polychronic time is a system in which several things can be done at the same time; it's a more fluid approach. This is common in southern Europe, in Latin and Arab cultures, as well as in India. Relationships are given more importance and there is less attention to time accounting.

If you visit a friend with a polychronic time culture and for some reason they are late for an appointment, it is hardly given importance because the relationship is what matters. You don't see the insult of being late that you would in a monochrome culture.

Continuing with the preferences of others, let's now turn to the topic of interactions. There are people oriented to the past, present or future. If a person is focused on the future, then he will give it more importance than the present or the past. They are good at planning, they are goal oriented, they have higher averages or grades, they save money, they may delay gratification, and they surely control the ego.

They can also be people who enjoy current activities less, are less affectionate with those around them, relate everything that is happening to what has already happened. They are people who operate from a negative past, positive perspectives on yesterday, and base their perspectives on these experiences.

A person oriented to the past has had sad, painful or traumatic experiences, issues that have not been overcome, they are more pessimistic and expect less from the future, they even hesitate to dare.

Present-oriented people can be divided into two categories: hedonistic or fatalistic. When they are fatalists they think that fate is in charge of their lives, so they live passively, they think they have no power.

In the case of hedonists, they enjoy life more, are impulsive, spontaneous and take risks. They get lost in the emotions of the moment and live passionate relationships.

Someone's orientation to time determines what we learn from them, what we decide to say to them, and what might be possible in a relationship with them.

Discovery Activity: How to Explore Someone's Inner World

Let's have a little fun with this. Complete these questions to see what you already know about someone:

Person:

How is it related to time?

When they make a description, especially experiences, what does the language tell you about the representation system in which they are processing?

Are they more visual, auditory, or kinesthetic?

What metaprograms do you notice in the behavior?

What is the orientation ?:

- Options or procedures?
- Towards or away from?
- Proactive or reactive?
- Internal or external?
- General or specific?
- Coincidence or mismatch?

How would you classify the content domains of the metaprogram: people, place, information, activities, and things?

How would you imagine that they would complete the sentences?

Am _____.

People are _____.

Life is _____.

What beliefs do you notice that they say quite often?

Are these beliefs empowering or limiting?

These are just a starting point. As you interact with the identified person, you will see them with different eyes. You have to be curious and ask questions about missing information that would normally have been completed. As you come up with the information, identify which observations were correct and which were not.

The experience you lived will allow you to observe and question others. You will realize what is missing in communication and preferred internal representation.

Metaprograms help you understand and appreciate the internal world, both yours and that of others. Nobody has a bad way, it is just different, the differences reflect the richness of the human experience.

Conclusion

Now what's next with NLP?

It has been a journey, now we must quickly reflect on some things and relive the path that we covered together.

What have you learned so far?

Throughout this process you have learned about:

- Key assumptions of NLP
- How you "work" using your body, brain and mind
- The way you use the five senses to process, classify and store your experiences.
- How to notice the incongruity in yourself and in others.
- How your mind uses an abbreviation to assimilate, filter, make sense and manage incoming data.
- The power of intentional and unintentional visual, auditory, and kinesthetic anchors.
- You discovered the subtle changes in the sub-modalities and how they can create great changes in your now.
- The importance of where you are in the experience, whether you are associated or dissociated.
- Non-verbal behaviors that can provide clues to what is happening with another person and shape who they are in the world.

- Ways to create good connections with others by building an easy relationship, showing interest, and making them feel good.
- The systems of representation, sense of time, metaprograms, etc., serve to communicate effectively.
- The power of beliefs and how each individual's beliefs shape their experience, decisions, interactions, and identity.
- How conflicts occur and how to increase collaboration to enjoy relationships more and have better results.
- Changing submodalities
- How to persuade and influence others with NLP techniques
- Language patterns with great persuasive power.

Next steps to continue with NLP

You are finishing this book, you could close it and forget about it or continue to improve your life and achieve more. I encourage you to consider this:

Explore NLP, establish an excellent base for you to make personal changes, take advantage of this, instead of looking for the next book or online course, you can delve into NLP and see how to use it more with the information you already have in this issue.

The more you learn about NLP, the more you can apply it to yourself and the more options you will have to make successful changes in yourself and in your life. If you've taken notes throughout the book, you may already have a list of things you want to change.

Learning NLP has provided you with information about personal thought patterns and has helped you manage them as you wish. If you have ways of dealing with other people and you want to change them or if you want to understand how they are thinking and feeling, then NLP is perfect for you. These tools will serve the path that awaits you.

I hope you have an exciting journey, filled with many rewards. I thank you for having allowed us to live this experience together, where I hope you finished a little wiser than when you began to read the first page.

Thanks

Dear reader, thank you very much for reaching the end of this book.

If you liked the content and consider that you have learned something interesting that can improve your life, I would be very grateful if you could leave me an assessment about it.

It would mean a lot to me and it would help me to continue providing valuable content to the community =)

Thank you!

If you are interested in other books with similar themes to communication and influence, I leave you the links so that you can access them. Do not miss the opportunity to learn everything about hypnotic communication and persuasion in depth:

Made in the USA
Columbia, SC
17 December 2021